Murders and Moralities

MURDERS
AND
MORALITIES
ENGLISH
CATCHPENNY PRINTS
1800-1860

Thomas Gretton

A Colonnade Book

Colonnade Books
are published by British Museum Publications Ltd and are
offered as contributions to the enjoyment, study and
understanding of art, archaeology and history.

The same publishers also produce the official publications of
the British Museum.

British Library Cataloguing in Publication Data

Gretton, Thomas
  Murders and moralities.
  1. Broadsides   2.   Street literature –
  England
  I. Title
  398.5   PR967

ISBN 0–7141–8028–9

Published by British Museum Publications Ltd,
6 Bedford Square, London WC1B 3RA

Designed by James Shurmer

Set in Times New Roman and
printed in Great Britain by Butler and Tanner Ltd,
Frome and London

Cover: Crim con extraordinary published by J. Paul, early 1840s

Contents

Acknowledgments

I should like to thank Antony Griffiths and
Frances Carey, Assistant Keepers of the
Department of Prints and Drawings in the British
Museum, who encouraged me to begin, and to
Robert Hatch, who read and commented on the
text.

I am also grateful to the staff of the following
libraries, from which this collection derives, for
their kind permission to reproduce photographs.

Bodleian Library, Oxford: 5, 10, 14, 16, 17, 19,
26, 32, 44, 45, 54, 56, 66, 67, 68, 69, 88, 93

British Library: 1, 6, 15, 22, 23, 27, 41, 48, 49,
50, 51, 53, 64, 72, 73, 76, 78, 86, 89, 91, 92

British Museum: 30, 34, 35, 36, 39, 40, 42, 43,
46, 47, 57, 58, 59, 60, 61, 62, 63, 65, 84

Guildhall Library: 9, 11, 25, 31, 33, 70

St Bride Printing Library: 2, 3, 4, 7, 8, 12, 13,
18, 20, 21, 24, 28, 29, 37, 38, 52, 55, 71, 74, 75,
77, 79, 80, 81, 82, 83, 85, 87, 90

Introduction

During the course of the nineteenth century the quality and quantity of visual information available to the industrialising world underwent a profound transformation. In the fifteenth century the development of printing from etchings, engravings and woodcuts had made it possible to reproduce images accurately. Technological changes in the nineteenth century ensured that such information became available to all. These changes, while making possible such radically new media as the *Illustrated London News* or the *Graphic*, also destroyed old forms of communication. Among these were the etched caricatures of Gillray and Cruikshank, and the illustrated ballads and broadsides which had been sold on city streets and in country markets for 200 years. Instead of simply fading away in the face of this new competition, however, the ballad and broadside trade reacted with vigour and ingenuity, especially in the years from 1820 to 1850. Indeed, so well were old forms and traditional preoccupations adapted to new demands that up to 250,000 copies of some broadsides were sold.

As well as the intrinsic interest which the swan-song of an ancient form may afford, there is a wider context in which ballads and broadsides are particularly important. We can catch a glimpse of the way in which men of the past visualised the world only by considering the images they have left behind. For the most part only oil paintings, fine prints and sumptuously illustrated books produced by a highly skilled and esteemed élite for a small and powerful group of well-educated and worldly people have survived to attract our attention. Consequently, it is the tradition of imagery associated with the collections of the rich that has been the strongest influence in determining our view of the past. Nineteenth-century ballad and broadside imagery documents another way of seeing: it not only affords an understanding of what the less privileged expected from pictures but also reflects the kind of world they lived in and their attitude towards it.

The prints in this book have been selected to show how the relationship between image and information in the ballad and broadside developed and changed during the transitional years of the first half of the nineteenth century. This book does not present newly discovered material; it shifts the focus away from the texts and concentrates on the illustrations. In the past broadside imagery has been noted either for its blithe gruesomeness, as in Richard Altick's *Victorian Studies in Scarlet* (1972), or because it is so loosely connected with the text, a point raised but not investigated in L. Shepard's *The Broadside Ballad* (1962). In *Print and the People 1819–1851* (1976) Louis James presents a variety of material, including broadsides, but although he provides examples of eye-catching illustrations, he is primarily concerned with the texts. This modern emphasis reflects the bias of nineteenth-century Victorian investigators, such as Henry Mayhew, and of collectors, whose interest was more often aroused by the texts than by the job lots of crude and misplaced woodcuts with which the texts were bedecked.

It was inevitable, therefore, that the major collections of nineteenth-century broadside imagery found their way into libraries rather than into museums and art galleries. Most of the material on which this book is based is held by the British Library, the Guildhall Library, the St Bride Printing Library and the Bodleian Library; but it is the miscellany of prints held by the Department of Prints and Drawings in the British Museum, in the 'English Caricature' series and elsewhere, that prompts a challenge to the predominantly literary interest in the ballad and broadside.

Before discussing the history and significance of broadside imagery, a word about terms is necessary. There is no English equivalent of *imagerie populaire*, as the French call this sort of material. 'Catchpenny print' was the label given to it at the time, mostly by those who held it in contempt. 'Street literature', as Henry Mayhew called it, lays stress on the verbal rather than the visual aspects of the material. 'Broadside imagery' is perhaps more appropriate, since single sheets, printed on one side only, were known as broadsides. Throughout the book individual broadsides are frequently referred to as 'sheets' and individual illustrations as 'cuts', both words being in common usage during the broadside's heyday.

In the eighteenth century broadsides had been peddled at executions, and ballad sheets and moral prints like *The Pilgrim's Progress* or *King Charles' twelve good rules* had been hawked on city streets, at country fairs, at markets and in inns. News of victories, disasters and political.controversies had been the subject matter not only of expensive caricatures and scarce newspapers but of the pedlars' stock-in-trade, sometimes in the form of special second editions of newspapers, sometimes of crude copies after Gillray, sometimes of topical ballads. Accordingly, nineteenth-century forms – the slip ballad, the murder, trial or execution sheet, the comic dialogue, the political cartoon, the moral tale or the collection of evangelical hymns and prayers – all have eighteenth-century ancestors.

In purely physical terms nineteenth-century broadside images were innovative in two crucial respects: they were produced from wood-engravings; and they were printed on cast-iron presses, a combination which could produce abundant, cheap and finely detailed prints. Wood-engravers use the end-grain of a hard and dense wood (usually box) to work on, whereas woodcuts, the most common eighteenth-century technique, are made from a plank with the design cut from the length of the grain. Both methods produce a block where the area cut away leaves no impression and the area in relief prints black. Printers had used end-grain blocks even in the seventeenth century, but it was only after Thomas Bewick had developed and popularised the technique in superbly illustrated books published between 1790 and 1804 that wood-engraving became the rule.

Previously, illustrations had for the most part been printed either from wood-cuts, which are relatively easy to make but which cannot carry such fine detail as wood-engravings, or from etchings and engravings. These employ the intaglio technique in which ink is smeared on to the flat surface of a metal plate and then rubbed off. The lines and pits cut into the plate hold the ink residue and print black, leaving the unengraved area white. Intaglio plates are capable of repro-ducing fine tonal and linear detail with great accuracy. Unfortunately, printing from them is a skilled and laborious exercise, unlike the relatively straight-forward job of printing woodcuts or wood-engravings, and the finer the print being produced, the more quickly the plate wears out. While wood-engravings, like woodcuts, can print hundreds of thousands of copies, even relatively crude intaglio plates are probably not good for more than a few hundred copies with-out considerable reworking. Wood-engraving offered the advantages of both the principal eighteenth-century reproductive techniques: it yielded fine lines and accurate detail; and it made long print runs possible.

A knowledge of printing techniques aids in an understanding of the ante-cedents and evolution of nineteenth-century broadside imagery. With some exceptions, eighteenth-century woodcut illustrations had been coarse in detail and careless of topographical or historical accuracy; they were so generalised that one woodcut could, and often did, serve on many occasions in a variety of ways. Intaglio illustrations, on the other hand, were precise, specific and accu-rate, and since they wore out quickly, new ones were usually produced to meet each new occasion. A concern for uniqueness, originality and specificity was therefore associated in the eighteenth century with high costs and small editions. Imagery produced in this way was available to the rich, and at second hand to their servants and hangers-on. Wood-engraving, however, made it possible for accurate and specific visual reporting to be enjoyed by a much larger audience. In the end this new technology proved better suited to other media, and the broadside, the carrier of a repetitive and generalised form of imagery, perished despite vigorous and, in the short term, successful efforts to adapt.

Many factors combined to offer the broadside its Indian summer. General changes played their part: a rising population, its growing wealth and literacy, its concentration in cities and its increasing involvement in politics and the life of the nation as a whole. There were also specific influences at work: the legal and fiscal restrictions placed on newspapers, the changing class structure of the news-vending trade and various technological and commercial transformations in the printing industry. The general changes tell us why popular literature was commercially successful during the period. There were more people, living in larger cities, with, by and large, more money to spend, and old types of play, such as prize-fighting, cock-fighting and bull-baiting, were in increasingly bad odour as 'brutal' rather than 'rational' recreation. In the circumstances new forms of more private recreation naturally developed, and success came to appropriate old ones.

The broadside and the ballad did not, however, prove to be appropriate old forms for long. The first reason why they succeeded for a while in exploiting a growing and changing market was that the new market did not emerge overnight; it grew slowly and unsteadily as prosperity and literacy both hesitantly advanced. Pre-existing cultural forms had time, therefore, to adapt to changing conditions. The second reason was that for a while legal, commercial and technological conditions actually favoured the broadside. Stamp duty had first been introduced on newspapers in 1712 but had been raised several times during and after the Napoleonic Wars until during the 1820s 4d of *The Times* price of 7d was duty. In theory any printed paper which dealt with news had to pay the duty, but in practice it was levied only on regular periodicals dealing with political news. Ballads and broadsides, almost by definition, were not periodical publications, and as long as their subject matter was not political – or if political, not conspicuously radical – the duty could safely be evaded. This gave broadsides a clear commercial advantage over their natural competitors, cheap newspapers, which laboured under a crucial handicap until the abolition of the 'tax on knowledge' in 1855.

This boost from the taxman undoubtedly increased the broadside's appeal to its consumers, but it does not explain what made broadsides attractive to their producers. In fact, they were produced by only a few printers: in London fewer than a dozen firms, with two or three predominant, were active at any one time; and in provincial centres like Birmingham, Bristol or Newcastle there were one, two or perhaps three printers active simultaneously. Such a printer would live, and sometimes get rich, by skilfully combining different sorts of trade. The slow and steady production of slip ballads, chapbooks and old favourites like *The twelve stages of human life* (78) would be spiced with hectic and unpredictable bursts of printing activity triggered by a bloody or high-society murder, a disaster or a political controversy. Sensational stories like the *Red Barn Murder* (in modern tabloid terms: 'Maria's Buried in Barn, Dreams Mother. Missing Playboy Accused') would provoke a demand which the specialist printers were unable to meet from their own presses, and they would farm the extra work out to jobbing printers.

Such printing flexibility could be achieved only if the items to be sold required relatively little typesetting (making it easy to increase the number of presses printing the same item) and only if the presses used could adapt to a changing rhythm and a wide variety of work. An astute combination of long and short runs, quick and slow runs, had provided the pattern of successful print-shop management in the eighteenth century. With the development during the first half of the nineteenth century of specialised powered presses to deal with long high-speed print runs, the newspaper, book and jobbing printing trades diverged. The scale and pace of technological innovation greatly increased the capital necessary to run a competitive print-shop, at the same time limiting the sorts of work which such a shop would be equipped to undertake.

The ballad and broadside trade offered a few printers the freedom to exploit a growing market while clinging to old management techniques, old equipment, old sorts of product and the old level of capital investment. The major disadvantage of such a way of trading – varying run lengths on hand-presses – was that a good deal of skilled labour was required. Accordingly, every effort was made to cut costs. Careless and unskilled compositors were often employed, proofreading was neglected, blocks of type were kept standing even after they had been jumbled up or knocked about, and, by the 1850s at least, stereotypes of unchanging items were taken and stock printed from them as necessary. The mechanical presses which were introduced after 1814 threw a steady stream of skilled hand-pressmen on to the labour market, and while this proletarianising of the printing industry was going on, the ballad and broadside trade was assured of cheap skilled labour whenever it was needed. For the printer, then, this trade offered the chance to produce a commodity with a steady sale and a low unit cost at a nominal capital outlay, and to cash in on the occasional boom in demand without increasing either investment or permanent overhead.

Because the ballad and broadside trade was a humble one whose success was short-lived, our knowledge of the men who ran it is rather limited. However, James Catnach, one London broadside printer, was fortunate in having an enthusiastic nineteenth-century biographer, Charles Hindley, so we know a little about his fortunes and working methods. Catnach began his celebrated career after pushing a handcart loaded with a wooden press and some second-hand type away from Northumberland and his bankrupt father's creditors. After his retirement in 1838 his shop passed to his sister, Ann Ryle, and her associate, James Paul. William Fortey took the business over during the 1850s and for a while traded on nostalgia, calling himself 'William Fortey, at the Catnach Press, the oldest and cheapest house in the world for ballads and broadsheets'. During the 1870s he changed his imprint, calling himself 'steam printer'.

John Pitts, whose shop at the wholesale toy and marble warehouse was close to Catnach's in Seven Dials, was probably at least as prolific as his rival. He ran a firm whose antecedents, stock, and collection of woodblocks derived from the London ballad trade of the seventeenth century. The most interesting of the other London printers who worked in Seven Dials was Thomas Birt, readiest of all to provide accurate and sophisticated cuts. Another major concentration, especially from the 1840s onwards, was around Brick Lane in Spittalfields, and there were printers also in Hackney, the City, Southwark and Soho.

Broadside and ballad printers in the provinces, in Bristol, Norwich, Lincoln, Newcastle upon Tyne, Birmingham, Oxford and elsewhere, traded throughout the period, but their range of products, and presumably the size of their markets, was more restricted than those of their London counterparts from whom they 'borrowed' successful subjects.

Little information has survived about the commercial fortunes of these men, though we know that Catnach had acquired four wooden presses by 1821 (later they were surely replaced by cast iron) and that, according to Hindley, he retired £30,000 richer than he was when he arrived in London in 1812. This is not enormous wealth, but it does represent an outstanding rate of return on a business with a fixed capital probably never greater than £300 or £400. Moreover, Catnach neither worked nor saved obsessively: indeed, it seems he had plenty of time to drink and to buy his friends drinks.

We have seen in general terms why broadsides were attractive to purchasers and why they suited a small group of printers so well: but what had they to offer the people who sold them? Ballads and broadsides could be sold in a variety of ways: some printers sold them retail, and they were to be found in a few toyshops and bookshops; the overwhelming majority, however, were sold by pedlars and hawkers, both in the town of origin and further afield.

Henry Mayhew's detailed account of the sellers of street literature in *London Labour and the London Poor* divides them into distinct trades: running patterers, standing patterers, buskers, chaunters and 'mere traders'. Those in the first four categories drummed up trade through some sort of performance. The running patterers, specialists in hot news of the disaster and execution sort, would sell on the move, in parties, making as much stir as possible in the street or market that they were working. Standing patterers would pick a good spot and stay there, selling less sensational items – comic dialogues, lives of heroes and rehashes of famous events. Buskers sold both these classes of sheet round inns and taverns rather than in the open air. Chaunters worked indoors or out, singing the ballads which they hoped to sell. Mayhew tells us little of the 'mere traders' who sold slips and sheets without fuss or performance or of the way the country trade, as opposed to that of London, was organised.

In the country, as well as in London, retail sellers of slips and sheets worked for profit, not for wages. They would buy sheets from the printer or wholesaler in lots of six, a dozen, or more, at about half the retail price. Lots of a gross or more carried larger discounts but would be difficult for itinerant sellers to finance, transport or store. It seems likely that both retailers and wholesalers specialised in one particular 'line'. Catnach frequently put 'travellers and country shops supplied' on his religious broadsides, while on murder and execution sheets he advertised his services as a printer of cards and invoices, objects of more interest to town customers. Provincial wholesalers who bought regularly from a printer might arrange to have their names listed on his sheets as stockists.

Given the high rate of profit, why did bookshops not sell broadsides and ballads retail as well as wholesale? The answer must be that bookshops were unable to attract the sort of customer who might buy them. If we turn the question round and ask why ballads and broadsides were so attractive to pedlars, the answer is more complex. The high rate of profit on each sale was an important reason, but there were others. Like the nineteenth-century broadside, itinerant trading was in a period of transition. In the eighteenth century a very wide variety of articles had been available in many areas of the country only from pedlars or travelling market-traders. As towns grew, so did the number and variety of retail shops, and the empire of the wandering traders shrank. Pedlars and hawkers concentrated on those goods not yet sold in shops and on buyers too poor, too isolated or too inexperienced to buy in them.

Besides this general tendency, there was an important specific change. Newsmen, the itinerant distributors of newspapers who at the end of the previous century had, like other street vendors, been their own masters and traded for their own profit, were by 1840 much more likely to be employed to deliver papers or, at best, to sell them for a wage. It seems likely, therefore, that the ballad and broadside trade offered a refuge in particular to those sellers of street literature who wanted to work for themselves, and in general to pedlars driven from other lines by the development of shop-based commerce.

Henry Mayhew offers much the best account of the organisation of ballad and broadside selling in the late 1840s. In general this account can be taken to hold for the whole of the period covered in this book. Throughout his discussion on street-selling Mayhew stresses that some specialisations spring up to exploit a novelty and then decline. This process may be true of some of the specialisations described above. One becomes conscious of the tension between an ancient form with an old-established commercial organisation and the growing necessity of finding new content and selling it in new ways.

If notions about the printers and sellers of these sheets are vague, knowledge about their buyers is even sketchier. It seems clear that while some broadsides were bought by the rich and well-educated the great majority were sold to the relatively poor and ignorant. Within London one sort of material would be sold to the servants of Mayfair, another to the artisans of St Giles or Spittalfields. There is little evidence to show that ballads and broadsides were bought by people who had access to their more sophisticated equivalents; when the rich did buy them it was out of curiosity, or as a souvenir of a hanging. They were bought instead by people whose access to other literary or pictorial forms was restricted by geography, culture or money – perhaps by all three.

Ballads and broadsides came in a variety of forms. The most important eighteenth-century form had been the slip ballad, printed on one side of the paper and measuring about 250 mm by 100 mm (height here and elsewhere in the book precedes width). Before the application of cast-iron technology to printing, these dimensions had represented one-eighth of a printed sheet. The cast-iron hand-presses developed in the first quarter of the century printed a larger area more accurately, and the perfection of mechanical paper-making by the end of the 1820s meant that the greater capacity of the new hand- and machine-presses could be made use of when required. Nevertheless, the ballad and broadside trade continued to produce objects of roughly eighteenth-century dimensions, perhaps partly because the 'whole sheet' was the largest size that could conveniently be displayed in a crowded and blustery street or market.

The slip ballad was the smallest item regularly printed. Next came the quarter sheet, about 250 × 200 mm; half sheets were roughly 400 × 250 mm; full sheets about 500 × 400 mm. Occasionally a collection of ballads would be sold on a sheet halved lengthways. Nineteenth-century ballad printers made the most of their capacity for printing larger sheets only when they produced 'yards' of ballads, sheets 900 × 250 mm, with verses printed in three long columns. Sometimes two or three of these 'yards' would be pasted end to end, and a sheaf of them pinned to a pole – Mayhew illustrates one pedlar using this method of attracting trade. Ballads and broadsides were almost always printed on the cheapest paper available, which, especially before the coming of the paper-making machines, was often very coarse indeed. Exceptionally a religious print would advertise the fact that it could be bought on fine paper at twice the price.

Broadside and ballad illustrations have many affinities with their typography. This combines careless, penny-pinching expedience with a slow acceptance of the need to modernise and meet higher standards. Founts of type were usually bought second-hand, and one seldom finds a ballad or a broadside, especially an early one, that is not printed from more or less battered type. Mixed founts were often used to print a text – little effort was made to keep typefaces from getting jumbled. If, as was often the case, there proved to be too much matter for the space available, a much smaller face might be used for the last column or part of a column, and the change would sometimes occur in mid-sentence. When such expedients did not answer, the narrative would simply stop, again, if necessary, in mid-sentence, when the space ran out.

Despite this chaotic and lackadaisical approach, the typography of broadsides did undergo a transformation during the period. Thanks to the increased pressure and accuracy with which cast-iron presses worked, it became possible to design typefaces that combined large areas of black, difficult to print without great pressure, with delicate and fine lines, which are easily damaged if excessive force is applied. This new flexibility changed the appearance of both text and display founts. In particular, the variety and boldness of the new display faces were quickly exploited for the titles of ballads and the headlines of broadsides.

Layouts for ballads and broadsides were in general very simple, with the title either preceding or following the illustration at the top and the text filling most of the sheet. The larger the size, the more variations are to be found. Full sheets, especially those on religious themes, sometimes carried decorative borders, which also appear, more rarely, on half sheets. Half-sheet texts would be set in from one to three columns, full sheets in from one to five. Full sheets, like half and quarter sheets, would be dominated by a large cut at the top, although there would probably be additional illustrations in the text. In the case of execution sheets these might include portraits of the murderer or his victim, pictures of the scene of the crime and courtroom or gaol scenes. Religious sheets, especially hymn sheets, show the greatest variation. Individual hymns might be set in compact two-column blocks, with the page considerably broken up by illustrations, dominated, perhaps, by a bust of Christ or the Crucifixion at the centre of the sheet. Unlike the etched cartoons of Gillray or Cruikshank, few ballads or broadsides were coloured, and when they were, they were tinted in a limited range of colours applied in broad blotches that made little attempt to follow the black and white image.

It is on ballad slips that one finds the oldest blocks being used, and the same blocks being reused most often. Frequently this sort of block is worm-eaten or so filled with fluff and old ink that it prints hardly any detail. Some of them, on the evidence of the costumes, date from the late seventeenth century. Almost all the cuts are unsigned – perhaps only half a dozen signatures are to be found among the thousands of distinct images that have survived. Among the signatures are those of two printers, J. V. Quick and D. H. Carpue, whose blocks were by no means used exclusively by themselves.

Hindley suggests that Catnach not only wrote the prose texts and verses for some of his sheets but also, when the need arose, cut the blocks. It seems likely that most of the cuts were designed and executed by a single hand, whereas in papers such as *Punch* or the *Illustrated London News* one man might provide a sketch, one man would draw the illustration, another transfer the drawing to the boxwood block and another, or team of others, do the cutting. Broadside printers could employ wood-engravers who were more and more highly skilled, but the prints never show any evidence that they employed skilled draughtsmen, let alone people with an academic training in the fine arts.

A comparison of the form and the subject matter of broadsides exposes one marked contradiction: the most immediate, the most novel, the most newsy subject matter – the murder sheet – was presented in the most conservative way, while the eternal verities of religion were treated with panache and originality. The broadside demonstrated and tried to resolve the tension between continuity and change, between eternal and reportorial truths. Its subject was either a changeless aspect of the human condition or unique and unrepeatable. Useful, generally applicable information of a concrete sort was largely absent from the form. The subject matter of ballads, for example, included themes of love, death, drink, homesickness and mythic heroism. Only towards the end of the period, and chiefly in sheets printed in the north of England, does one find many examples of songs about immediate events, such as battles, public affairs or public men, sold as slip ballads.

Religious subjects and moral sheets often told a supposedly true story, such as the one of a merchant's daughter who was seduced and abandoned by a naval officer, sank to prostitution, thence to theft, was transported, served her time, was shipwrecked on the way home, and after further vicissitudes was reunited with her aged and at last forgiving parent. Though the circumstances were modified to suit each market, the story remained the same from printer to printer: the eternal triumphed over the temporal. Comic sheets and dialogues, even when triggered by something as specific as the Marriage Act of 1823, which altered the age of consent and the law relating to Gretna Green weddings, exploited changeless themes. One striking exception was the successful *Tom and Jerry* series sold by Catnach in the early 1820s. Tom and Jerry, rich youths up from the country and sampling high and low life in the capital, had first appeared in Pierce Egan's *Life in London* in 1821. In both the Egan and the plagiarised Catnach versions emphasis is laid on precise social observation and topical jokes. Neither its text nor its imagery, which considerably influenced later broadside humour, had antecedents in the form.

'Cocks', as the trade called them, were another important variety of sheet. They were reports of fake events – imaginary tragedies, scandals, monstrosities, even bogus murders and executions. When they were illustrated, cuts which had done prior service were almost always used. Cocks were usually rather small, quarter or sometimes half sheets, presumably because those who worked them had to move fairly quickly from one market to the next. The success of such sheets exposes the ambiguous news value of 'news' broadsides: cocks carried conviction not because they heaped up circumstantial detail but because they employed the same formulae as sheets concerning real murders, tragedies or scandals. This suggests that both sorts of sheet sold more because they offered the familiar than because they offered the new.

The range of subject matter covered by genuine 'news' broadsides was narrow. With the major exception of the agitation that led to the 1832 Reform Bill, when riots were reported and the imagery of intaglio political caricature was relayed by men such as Catnach and Pitts to their markets, straight political controversy seldom evoked broadsides. Politics most commonly occurred in conjunction with religious prejudice, royal death or scandal, or highly ritualised events like elections. Recurrent disasters such as shipwrecks were always popular, as were standardised accounts of another form of ritualised contest, the prize-fight. Occasionally a major innovation – the opening of the new London Bridge, the introduction of steam-carriages, the Great Exhibition – evoked a broadside, but by far the largest group of 'news' broadsides dealt with murder.

Henry Mayhew details the way a first-rate murder could be made to yield a series of sheets, beginning with the discovery of the body and normally ending with the execution of the guilty party, and Richard Altick has discussed the sensibility behind the public fascination with murder. Here it is worth noting some oddities about the murder-trial-execution sequence when viewed as an event. Every murder is evidently unique and cannot happen again; but murder is a form of death, the irrevocable end of uniqueness. Trials and executions are highly ritualised and convert the unique and unfamiliar into the familiar and the recurrent. The murder sheet, which of all the broadside repertoire seems to be most closely concerned with the here and now, therefore indicates the hesitation and ambivalence with which the form played its role as purveyor of information. The point is underlined by the fact that murder sheets, in their texts and in their images, were highly standardised and followed familiar formulae.

So much, then, for the origins and role of the broadside. It remains to discuss the sources, internal logic and cultural or historical significance of the cuts themselves, what influences and traditions shaped these images, how they work in their own terms, and what importance we might grant them today.

Attempts to find the sources of many of the surviving images are, at least at present, futile. Much of the material has been scattered or destroyed; much that survives is not only undated but undatable. We can, however, identify three main types of influence: a legacy of forms and images from eighteenth-century ballads and broadsides; the adoption of successful broadsides by competing printers; and innovations derived from other forms of imagery, both past and contemporary.

The ballad and broadside trade of the nineteenth century was much more extensive than that of the previous century, and it is possible that after a period at the end of the seventeenth century and the beginning of the eighteenth, when many broadside and ballad images were created, there had been only a slow enlargement of the repertoire. Perhaps the greatest legacy which nineteenth-century broadside printers received from their forerunners was not so much the tradition of a specific style of imagery as the attitude of making do, of letting one image do duty on countless occasions. As a result, nineteenth-century ballad printers frequently, and printers of news and religious sheets occasionally, used eighteenth-century blocks.

The second source of broadside imagery was the trade itself. Copying was the rule; the scene of the gallows at Newgate looking north occurs in half a dozen or more closely similar versions; the prisoner solitary in his cell, *Death and the lady* and *The twelve stages of human life* in at least four. The adaptation of a successful sheet, even when it was not copied directly, resulted in the sharing not only of specific images but of visual styles and pictorial conventions.

Neither past achievement nor contemporary practice had so fertile nor for us so problematical an influence on the broadside repertoire as that of other forms of imagery. The scale and nature of such influence varied as the broadside evolved to meet changing circumstances, but it was never absent. The simplest way it made its presence felt was in the obvious preference of broadside printers for cheap blocks: damaged or outdated blocks from a periodical or a bankrupt printer's stock could be picked up for a song and used where at all appropriate. Catnach, for example, owned both some of Thomas Bewick's blocks and one of the *Raft of the Medusa* by Gericault. As more and more books and periodicals were illustrated with wood-engravings, more and more used blocks became available. It is hard to imagine how such images could find themselves not only in the same print-shop but on the same page as some of the more basic cuts produced from within the broadside trade, but they did so, and they must surely have modified the expectations of readers and printers alike.

Direct infiltration of blocks was not the only way in which 'higher' art forms had effect on the broadside. In religious sheets, in particular, one finds evidence of considerable familiarity with sixteenth- and seventeenth-century religious art, though it is hard to discover how such familiarity was achieved. When printers of religious sheets could find no apposite model to copy, their inventions increasingly showed an awareness of the symbolic conventions and iconography of high art.

Despite the considerable impression it made on religious broadsides, the high art of the past had less influence on the evolution of broadside imagery than did other forms, not of art but of illustration. Above all one notes conscious and unconscious echoes of the topical, topographical and satirical intaglio prints of the eighteenth and early nineteenth centuries and of the illustrated papers and magazines whose growing success dates from the late 1830s. Of these *Punch*, founded in 1841, and the *Illustrated London News*, founded in 1842, are the best known today, but they had a host of predecessors, rivals and imitators.

Illustrated papers can seldom have competed directly with the broadsides, at least until the lifting of the stamp duty, but they were none the less influential. First, they greatly increased the supply of skilled wood-engravers, as well as that of used wood-engravings. The broadside printers certainly profited from the latter, and the increasing technical competence of the cuts of the 1840s and 50s shows that they profited from the former too. Second, and less tangibly, these new media were harnessing sophisticated pictorial conventions to convey accurate visual information to a far wider audience than had previously been possible. Since newspapers were so expensive, cut-price methods of making them accessible were devised: there is evidence that copies of the *Illustrated London News* or the *Illustrated Times* and of other cheap illustrated papers such as the *Observer* were sometimes to be found in the sorts of pubs and coffee-houses frequented by the readers of broadsides and could thus influence their tastes and expectations.

This new form of imagery, produced by a highly capitalised mass-circulation press, was unlike that of the broadsides in two crucial respects: it set a premium on accurate and, where possible, first-hand visual reporting; and it employed techniques of representation and composition directly derived from fine art. Besides making a highly developed, powerful and flexible set of pictorial styles available, the illustrated magazines also presented a much wider variety of material, offering both news and features with a wealth of precise circumstantial detail. Broadsides responded not only by attempting to adapt their style of imagery but by widening their own repertoire and reprinting newspaper reports: by the 1850s train crashes and mine disasters, the Great Exhibition and the Crimean War had all become broadside subjects.

The other important influence was the tradition of caricature inherited from the eighteenth century and continued by such magazines as *Punch*. All the political cuts in this book, with the exception of one (44), demonstrate this influence above all others; but it was not only in political sheets that the effects of caricature became visible. Early in the period the crowd at executions had been presented in broadsides in a direct, unpatronising and relatively undistorted way. In 1864 we note a broadside illustrator using *Punch*-type caricatures of the poor to depict the same scene (20).

Until the end of the period broadside imagery managed to borrow what it wanted from the tradition of caricature without being taken over by it. With the new graphic reporting, on the other hand, there could be no safe borrowing, only resistance or capitulation. This can be explained on one level in commercial terms: intaglio caricature and its successors such as *Punch* were aimed at a market quite different from that of the broadside, while mass-circulation graphic reporting was, ultimately, aimed at the same one. It can also be explained in terms of visual style. The caricature makes its point with a combination of exaggeration and symbolic or emblematic representation. It does not aim at specific and accurate depictions but at some more general form of pictorial truth, and in this respect resembles the broadside. Intaglio caricature offers a more sophisticated but, in some respects, more limited version of the broadside's attitude to the visible world, and because there was no fundamental incompatibility between the two, borrowing between them raised few problems. Mass-circulation graphic reporting, however, confronts its viewer not with a limited convention but with a complete way of seeing the world, a way which seeks out, values and presents not generalised evocations but exact likenesses of people, places and events.

When one examines in detail the way the imagery of the broadside works, a tendency to generalise emerges as a constant feature. As we have already noted, the same cut is often used to illustrate several different events. This practice is most obvious in the case of executions but holds as well for murders, disasters, comic and moral sheets. One is often alerted to the presence of a recycled cut by an incongruity between text and image: the text specifies an open-air shooting, the illustration shows a corpse lying indoors with its throat cut; the text describes a tropical shipwreck, the cut shows boats setting out in a sea full of icebergs. Why was it assumed that an indoor knifing could do duty for an outdoor shooting, the aftermath of a mutiny for a Caribbean hurricane? The obvious answer would be that neither producers nor readers cared about the illustrations to these sheets, and that only the text counted. Indeed, it seems that in some slip ballads the mere presence of a cut was more important than what it represented. However, broadsides were illustrated more and more lavishly and with increasing care during the years from 1800 to 1860, and even early in the period the illustrations were markedly more profuse than they had been in the previous century. It is impossible to argue, therefore, that no one cared about the imagery.

Sometimes, of course, the images did illustrate the text precisely, but it was not necessary for them to do so to perform their crucial task. It seems that this task was not primarily the reporting of external facts but the triggering of associations and the arousal of emotions. Any image that provoked shock, horror or fright could serve to illustrate a murder sheet; any view of Newgate, however fragmentary, confused or insubstantial its depiction of the scene (provided it was correct in details of number and sex of the executed) could help to sell an execution sheet, even, at a pinch, an execution at a country gaol, because it could transmit a sense of the occasion.

Such an attitude could not coexist with the factual and technically sophisticated reporting style of the mass-circulation graphic newspapers. It was no longer sufficient to provide a standardised image which would move to shock, awe, fear or pity; when broadside printers presented a stock image – of a child murder, for example – as a believably specific action reported in a pictorially sophisticated way, the result could be unbearable (5). Immediate and credible portrayals of the extremes of madness, cruelty, despair and retribution were too strong to stomach, and the success of the illustrated papers in reporting the visible world with such impact therefore made the subject matter of broadside imagery unemployable.

One particular practice bears out this general point. Every printer had on hand a block of his local place of execution, with the space within the gallows cut out and a supply of hanged men and women ready to fit into the hole as the occasion dictated. In the earlier, more schematic cuts (17, 27) such a practice was in keeping with the rest of the image; but in a cut such as number 25, with its wealth of topographical and anecdotal detail, one notices, first, that the gallows itself has been made rather small and compositionally rather hard to spot, almost as though the illustrator were trying to spare us from the discomfort of too close a look, and, second, that the relationship between gallows, victim and background has forced the illustrator to substitute not a new corpse alone but a new slice of the whole scene. The effect is to sever the connection between the execution and its surroundings and to make a nonsense of the image. In the end the broadside's visual style was no more able to come to terms with that of mass-circulation graphic reporting than the broadside, as a medium, was able to compete with the illustrated papers.

History forgets losers, and broadsides, especially their imagery, have tended to be treated as curiosities: slightly quaint, rather charming, entertainingly gruesome. This dismissive attitude seems to us to be mistaken but it is understandable. Broadsides are not the obvious ancestors of any modern form of communication; their imagery stands at the head of no influential pictorial tradition. If broadside imagery is of interest today, then it must be not because it has been an influence on later forms but for its own sake, for what it can tell us about the world which gave it birth.

Nineteenth-century ballad and broadside imagery offers rich evidence about the kinds of pictorial representations which satisfied the vast majority of people who, even in wealthy, settled and well-educated England, had been excluded from sharing the visually sophisticated imagery of the élite, except by accident (in domestic service, for example) and in churches. Broadside imagery was not and never had been 'authentic' in the sense of being the untutored and spontaneous depiction of the world by the people for the people; it was the product of competitive commerce, not of folk art. However, the commercial system which produced it was adapted to serve a market whose experience of the world was essentially limited and unchanging. In the circumstances the most successful form of image was one which reduced the complex variety of the world to fit a restricted experience. Such reports and images had little ability to convey information but considerable power to evoke stock responses. In contrast with broadsides mass-circulation graphic reporting, whatever its shortcomings, assumed that its task was to expand its readers' experience and ability to embrace at least some of the visible complexities of this world.

As the experience of the audiences for broadsides changed, as material and social opportunities to experience new things multiplied during the nineteenth century, it was perhaps inevitable that an imagery whose strength lay in its ability to reduce multifarious experience to a restricted number of formulations should be replaced by one which sought always to increase knowledge of the visible world. The methods of the *Illustrated London News* so utterly destroyed the imagery of the broadside that it now requires some effort to see the latter as anything more than quaint and incompetent. This is not, after all, surprising: the history of broadside imagery confirms that the technological revolution has transformed not only the world we inhabit but the way we look at it, for ever eager for new sights and permanently dissatisfied with repetition.

Broadside imagery is now itself a novelty, and this book offers a range of unfamiliar images. However, perhaps the greatest novelty of all would emerge if we could use them to recapture the mental attitudes of a culture which neither welcomed nor was at ease with new ideas, people, places or activities. The broadside cut neutralised such changes by assimilating them into a slowly evolving repertoire of familiar, repetitive and derivative imagery.

List of Plates

Murders

Condemned Cells and Trials

Executions

News

Information

Politics

Humour

Ballads

Almanacks and Christmas Sheets

Moralities

Religion

Detail of Plate 43.

THE PLATES

In the captions that follow the place of publication is London unless otherwise specified. Dating ballads and broadsheets is a nightmare: sometimes murder and execution sheets give a date, and often one can discover from other sources when the events took place; but when history gives no clue, one is forced to rely on the address of the printer for a rough guide. Pitts, who worked from 1802 to 1841, moved his shop in 1819; Catnach, active from 1812 to 1838, enlarged his in 1834. One is clearly at a loss when no adequate printers' directories exist, or where the printer gives no name.

MURDERS

Illustrated murder sheets were usually
issued rather late in the sequence of
events from crime to punishment: the
discovery of the body might warrant a
plain quarter sheet, the arrest of a
suspect another. It was during the
process of committal, trial and
execution that the broadside murder
sheet came into its own. Its text would
rehash such evidence as was known,
and one cut would certainly illustrate
an aspect of the crime: the discovery of
the body, the murder itself and the
disposal of the body, especially if it
involved dismemberment. There would
frequently be a 'portrait' of the
supposed culprit, although for the most
part this was in fact an old block from
the printer's existing stock. In addition
there might be a topographical cut of
the scene of the crime. In a rural
murder this would also be a block from
stock; but for a murder in London
greater accuracy might be felt
necessary.

1 *Interesting trial of John Clewes, John Barnett and George Baines for the Oddingley murders*

Robert Heppel. Birmingham, 1830. 111 × 142 mm.

This full-sheet broadside is unusual in having three large cuts, of about equal size and importance, to illustrate different moments of this crime which, though committed during the Napoleonic Wars, did not come to light until 1830.

2 The Richmond tragedy

James Catnach. After 1834. 158 × 212 mm.

This cut and cut 3 are 'cocks', fake reports for sale in periods when news was dull. Both cuts combine details of a shocking murder with an affecting moral. This story, of how a youth brings the squire who had seduced and murdered his twin sister to justice, seems to have been reprinted from a chapbook. W. Kent in Newcastle published the same story with a very similar illustration.

3 The parents' crime, or fatal curiosity, an affecting and true history of the unnatural murder of James Harden, a young sailor

James Catnach. After 1834. 104 × 175 mm.

There were many versions of this story in which the parents kill their unknown guest for his money and recognise him, from a birthmark, as their son.

3

33

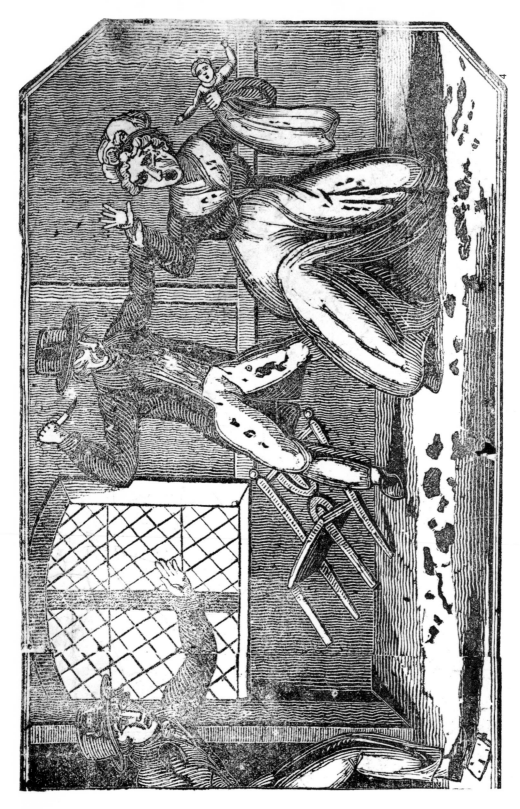

4 *Dreadful account of a most barbarous and shocking murder committed by William Burt upon the body of his infant child, and the cruel manner in which he wounded his wife at Brighton*

James Catnach. 1826. 158 × 245 mm.

Child murders sold well. This cut, which illustrates one of the more famous of them, had previously been used for another sheet and has been trimmed down the left-hand side. Catnach used it on another occasion, with a further 40 mm sliced off the left side, to illustrate a similar crime.

5

5 *Particulars of a mother murdering her infant child by dashing out its brains*

Thomas Birt. 86 × 135 mm.

Thomas Birt was one of the more successful of the broadside printers of the 1830s, producing rather more sophisticated illustrations than his rivals. Here the vigour and credibility of the cut combine with the horror of the action – a mother murdering her child while in prison – to produce an image whose gruesome vividness is almost too much to bear.

6 The Bristol Police Chronicle

J. Sherring. Bristol, 1837. 130 × 196 mm.

This cut is from one of the unstamped broadside papers of the late 1830s and seems out of place in its 'newspaper' setting. Notice the end-grain of the wood evident in the black areas: there are two blocks joined together and neither is of box; some less dense wood, perhaps oak, has been used instead.

7 Execution of John Stacey

James Catnach. 1829. 105 × 174 mm.

Since both cut and text emphasise that the murder weapon was a brick-hammer, it can be surmised that the block was done originally for this story; however, it was used frequently thereafter. From the text it appears that the right-hand scene preceded the left-hand one; the man who cut the block would have followed the normal comic-strip sequence, but the printing of the block of course reverses it.

MURDER

8 *Particular account of a most dreadful murder committed by Samuel Thorley upon the body of Ann Smith*

James Catnach. 1834. 86 × 162 mm.

The murderer, a butcher, ate the calf muscle of his victim, a ballad singer, out of professional curiosity.

9 *Latest particulars of the committal to Newgate of*
R. Gamble and M. Good, and confession of Daniel Good,
the murderer of Jane Jones

H. Paul. 1842. 150 × 136 mm.

Good burning the dismembered remains of Jane Jones was a popular moment
in this favourite murder. One newspaper illustrated the story with the all-
seeing eye of God present in each scene.

10

10 *Just published. The whole particulars of a most cruel murder committed by Charles Young, a grazier, upon the body of his sweetheart, Mary Ann Walmsley*

James Catnach. Before 1834. 75 × 134 mm.

This cut clearly shows the influence of the Bewick school, both in technical terms and in the idealised rural imagery which here combines so strangely with the scene of the shepherd finding the corpse.

11 *Life, trial, confession and execution of Richard Blakesley, executed at Newgate November 15th 1841, for the murder of Thomas Burdon, in Eastcheap*

Thomas Birt. 1841. 240 × 157 mm.

Blakesley's trial and execution sold a large number of broadsides. This one combines a relatively realistic and topographically accurate representation of the public house of which Burdon was landlord with a wooden and melodramatic representation of the fleeing culprit.

11

12 *The trial and execution of Capt. W. Moir for the murder of William Malcolm*

James Catnach. 1830. 112 × 197 mm.

Like child murders, killings involving members of the ruling class sold well. This cut is unusual in employing a 'speech bubble' like those regularly used by intaglio caricaturists.

CONDEMNED CELLS AND TRIALS

If execution sheets had more than a single illustration, the second one was most likely to be of the prisoner in his cell. Occasionally such scenes were given the place of honour. The prisoner was shown parting from his family, impassively or in anguish, writing his confession or a final letter (always printed below), alone with his guilt and his terror of the hereafter. Trials were less often depicted, and when they do occur they are illustrated very schematically.

13 *Execution and confession of J. Simpson, a boy, age 15, for robbing a dwelling house*

James Catnach. After 1834. 152 × 198 mm.

This had originally been a cut of the separation of a father from his wife and child, but the father has been hacked from the block and a praying youth appropriately inserted, which makes a nonsense of the wife and child.

14

14 *An account of the execution of John Williamson and W. S. Hetherington*

Gowland Summers. Sunderland, 1821. 79 × 62 mm.

This little cut comes from the head of an unusual single-column prose account of the same dimensions as a ballad slip. It was beautifully executed by a wood-engraver named Heavisides, who may have been trained by Bewick himself. Reproduced × 1.5.

15

15 *A particular account of James Cawthorne, who was executed on the Drop at Lincoln Castle, Thursday August 9 1821, for the murder of his wife*

W. Brooke. Lincoln, 1821. 51 × 100 mm.

This is a fine example of the most common formula for depicting the condemned man in his cell. Cruikshank drew on this tradition when he illustrated Fagin in his cell for *Oliver Twist*.
Reproduced × 1.2.

16 *Newgate Calendar*

John Pitts. 1824. 135 × 194 mm.

Courtroom scenes were common, especially on execution broadsides. Like execution scenes they derive more from one another than from direct observation. This cut is an unusually painstaking and detailed depiction of the interior of the Old Bailey.

EXECUTIONS

Execution sheets almost always featured a
gallows at their head. Depending on the
magnitude of the crime, they also gave portraits,
gaol scenes or reconstructions of the crime. Their
most striking feature was the gallows into which
the printer could drop a number of bodies.
Details of the number and sex of these executed
had to be correct. Other particulars mattered
less, though all the major printers had different
blocks for London, county-gaol and rural
hangings. Execution sheets gave a general view of
the scene rather than a close-up of the
condemned man.

17 *Execution of Henry John Naylor, George Adams, Edward Ward, George Anson, William Bartholomew, John Close, Edward Desmond, and John Davis*

J. Hughes. 1822. 104 × 147 mm.

This cut and cut 27 are two of many views of the Newgate gallows looking north, designed to take changing numbers of bodies. In this cut the view is clear and the crowd well observed; in the other, printed in Bristol for a Bristol execution, neither crowd nor architecture carries the same conviction. This cut is most unusual in that the number of bodies in the image is not the same as that in the text.

18 *The sorrowful and weeping lamentation of four lovely orphans left by J. Newton*

John Pitts. 1823. 139 × 192 mm.

This cut of a cart-tail hanging shows us a sharply observed crowd, with which the reader can easily identify, and even includes a woman selling execution sheets.

19 *The trials, executions and dying behaviour of of [sic] Thomas Cooper cutting and maiming Thomas Turner and John Fancutt, housebreaking*

James Catnach. 1816. 60 × 104 mm.

This early Catnach print retains many of the features of the Newgate Calendar, including a heavily mis-spelt confession. A gallows cut with a hole in it not being available, Catnach simply positioned the two extra corpses in mid-air.

Reproduced × 1.25.

20 *Trial and execution at the Old Bailey of seven seamen for murder and piracy on board the Flowery Land*

W. Fortey. 1864. 185 × 331 mm.

This sheet was printed and sold at the scene of the execution. Unfortunately, two of the pirates were reprieved, and a second edition, with two of the bodies cut out, was quickly produced. The comic-cartoon treatment of the faces of the crowd is interesting.

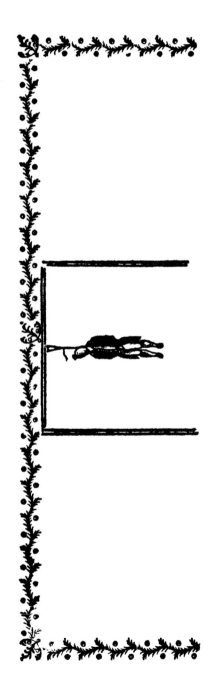

21 *Trial and sentence of James Nesbet who was executed this day,*
July 31, 1820, on Penmenden Heath

W. Epps. Rochester, 1820. 48 × 165 mm.

One drop-in corpse, three plain sets of parallel lines and some decorative borders are all that is necessary to convey this image.

22 *The execution of Wild Robert, being a warning to all parents*

J. Marshall. *c.* 1797. 82 × 101 mm.

This is one of the Cheap Repository Tracts, written by Hannah More and others to counteract inexpensive Jacobin propaganda and cheap sensational literature during the last decade of the eighteenth century. Most of the work which this group published was in pamphlet form, but there were also a few broadside tracts. This cut contains all the elements of a broadside execution illustration, but its pious atmosphere, its touching action, and above all the grace and fullness with which it is executed mark it as an imitation.

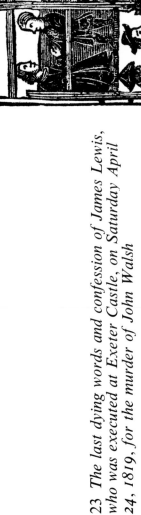

23 *The last dying words and confession of James Lewis, who was executed at Exeter Castle, on Saturday April 24, 1819, for the murder of John Walsh*

'Dewhirst, printer, Leeds, reprinted by J. Marshall Newcastle', 1819. 58 × 69 mm.

Used here in a long half sheet, this cut must originate before 1747 when Lord Lovat became the last man in England to be executed by beheading.

24 Just published – price 2d – an interesting and heart-rending account of a dreadful and unnatural murder committed by Jessy Dalton upon the body of her mother

James Catnach. Before 1834. 84 × 188 mm.
A cut of a rural execution, which was often reused.

25 *The life, trial and execution of R. Cooper*

'printed for the vendors', 1862.
144 × 289 mm.

This view of Newgate breaks with tradition in looking south and abandons the old emphasis on the gallows, giving us instead an accurate and detailed view of the crowd. The gallows and its occupant have, in contrast, been crudely cut and clumsily inserted.

26 *Trial, conviction and execution of Samuel Fallows, on 14th April 1823 at Chester*

John Atkinson. Barnard Castle, 1823. 49 × 64 mm.

This extraordinary design, copied presumably from some already highly stylised cut, reduces the elements of the hanging to an abstract pattern.

26

25

27 *An account of the last words and behaviour of four unfortunate men who were executed at Bristol on Friday January 27 1832*

John Bonner. Bristol, 1832. 66 × 144 mm.

These four men were executed as a result of their involvement in the Bristol Riots, part of the agitation preceding the Reform Bill. It is curious that while Bonner has thought it proper to use a cut of Newgate for a hanging which took place in Bristol the riot scene in the other cut on the sheet is unmistakably of the events in Bristol itself. The combination produces a curious blend of the specific political sheet and the generalised execution sheet, and the overall tone and presentation of the sheet tend to reduce the former to the latter.

NEWS

During the sixty years covered by this book a wide variety of general news stories found their way into the broadside repertoire. Throughout the period the favourite sort of story was of disaster, flood, shipwreck, fire or explosion. News of Britain, and of British ships and men, predominated. News broadsides very seldom carried more than a single large cut. As with most broadsides, printers would use an appropriate stock cut where possible, especially if they were in a hurry to get the sheet on the streets or doubted the news value of the story.

28 *Just published, the whole particulars of the dreadful shipwreck of the Cybelle*

James Catnach. 1834. 134 × 196 mm.

This is a good copy of Gericault's *Raft of the Medusa*, which had been exhibited in London in 1820. Probably done as part of the publicity surrounding that event, the block somehow found its way to Catnach.

29 *Dreadful shipwreck of the Francis Mary*

James Catnach. 1826. 190 × 340 mm.

This cut is unusual in bearing a lettered key, explained in the text.

Destruction of both Houses of Parliament by Fire,

30 The destruction of both Houses of Parliament by fire

James Catnach. 1834. 217 × 359 mm.

This is an accurate and striking image which is also interesting from a technical point of view. The small blocks of end-grain wood, which were bolted together to make a large image, are clearly distinguishable. The extensive black areas would have been impossible to print before the introduction of cast-iron presses and machine-made paper.

31 Destruction by fire of the Tower of London

Anne Ryle and James Paul. 1841. 104 × 177.mm.

The Tower fire is here represented by a close copy of a cut made by Woods to illustrate the Westminster fire of 1834.

31

32 *Wallsend explosion*

W. Kent. Newcastle, 1838. 186 × 218 mm.

Mine disasters were more frequently reported in broadsides after the end
of the 1830s. This cut accurately schematises the minehead and its railway.
Judging from the text, the block was in fact cut for an earlier disaster.

33 *Another dreadful suicide at the Monument*

E. lloyd. 1842. 153 × 142 mm.

Between 1839 and 1842 there was a spate of suicides from the Monument.
C. Paul, a printer at Seven Dials, even acquired a cut of the Monument
into which bodies of the appropriate sex could be dropped, as into an
execution block.

34 Great battle between the Russians and the French

Simms and McIntyre. Belfast; undated, but presumably 1812–14. 295 × 370 mm.

Battles were rarely made the subject of woodcuts, let alone of cuts as large as this one which is probably a copy of some engraving or etching of the battle of Borodino.

35 Most daring attempt to assassinate the Queen by John Francis

C. Paul. 1842. 108 × 226 mm.

This and a previous attempt on the life of the Queen evoked a variety of pictorial responses, from sophisticated topographical lithographs of the scene of the crime to this and even clumsier broadside illustrations. It is interesting to note that this attack was one of the first pieces of 'hot news' to be reported graphically in the *Illustrated London News*: though technically more skilled and artistically more competent, the *ILN* cut is perhaps not as assured as this one in its adoption of an appropriate visual style.

35

36 *Extraordinary exhibition at Saville House, Leicester Square*

Thomas Birt. 1834. 65×67 mm.

This is not so much an image illustrating a broadside for sale as a piece of street advertising. It was intended for the same public, however, and comes from a broadside printer.

INFORMATION

Occasionally broadside printers would abandon their
preoccupation with sudden death and the heareafter
and impart an unequivocally 'useful' item of
knowledge, or at least treat technological advance as
newsworthy. Such sheets are exceptional and may have
arisen from popular awareness of a controversy rather
than from an interest in technical innovation or
information for its own sake.

The New Invented Steam Carriage.

37

37 *The new invented steam carriage*

James Catnach. 1829. 315 × 183 mm.

Catnach perhaps obtained this cut from another source, since it is by no means in any of his usual styles. The letter-key in the image is explained in the text in a way which rather adds to the mystery. Note that some at least of the yokels are shown to be reacting with consternation and amazement at Mr Gurney's machines.

38 *A coal pit plan*

Undated, but probably 1830s. 385 × 297 mm.

This cut and that of a broadside in the Guildhall Library called *The Christian Collier*, whose image is almost identical, are unlike any others in the broadside repertoire. It is impossible to say which one came first – perhaps the print illustrated here is a more critical imitation of the other.

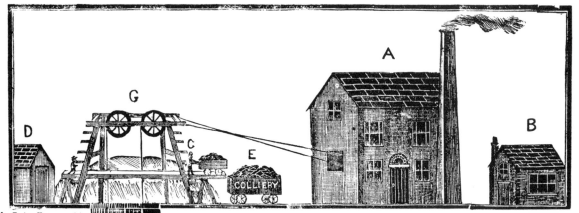

A.—Engine House, containing Engine for lifting the coal from the bowels of the earth to the surface.

B.—Pit Office, where safety-lamps are examined, and money paid to the miners.

C.—Banksman, empties the coal into the waggons.

D.—Hovel, where the Miners wait for their turn to descend the pit.

E.—Railway Waggon.

F.—Cage descending with two Miners.

G.—The Head Gear.

H.—Cage ascending with coal.

I.—Miners Holeing, or getting coal.

J.—Miners Curbing, or cutting coal.

K.—Miner Loading Coal into skep.

L.—Full Tubs being brought to the gate-road by horse and driver.

M.—Hanger-on, who puts the tubs on the cage to be sent above-ground.

N.—Man that rakes the gate-road to keep it clear.

O.—The Furnace that is kept burning at the bottom of the shaft for ventilation.

P.—Hurrier, with Tub, coming from the workings.

Q.—Driver with empty tubs.

R.—Hurrier bringing full tub to the main road.

S.—Miner Boarding.

T.—Miner at Long Work.

U.—The Sump, where the water of the mine is drained into before it is pumped to the surface.

V.—Man that mends the road.

W.—The Down Shaft.

X.—The Up Shaft.

Y.—The Pit Bank, where the coal is landed.

Z.—Safety Lamps, without which the Miners would not be able to work in pits where there is a large quantity of gas.

And Spurns and Spregs, which are left to support the roof.

THE dangers to which the Colliers are subject in Coal getting are many, and the awful sacrifice of life and limb, yearly, are at times appalling. The first great danger with which the Colliers have to contend is FIRE-DAMP; the second a FALL OF THE ROOF; and last but not the least, WATER, which not unfrequently breaks in and floods the mine. The Miners have a great many difficulties to encounter, and from the unhealthy nature of the work, as a rule their lives are short.

Dear Reader,—In a romantic village, in the RUNDER VALLEY, a sad pit accident occurred some time ago. Seventy-five men and boys went down that fatal shaft at the usual time of changing shifts. All went well till ten o'clock in the morning, when a terrible explosion took place in the pit, killing twenty-one men and boys and disabling many others for life by the loss of limbs. It is impossible to describe the scenes of agony and anguish at the pit's bank, as body after body was brought up, scarcely recognisable by the relatives or friends of the poor sufferers, who had thus so untimely met their death:

THE Christian Collier rises soon,
  With glory in his soul;
He prays he might be kept till noon.
  While working in the coal.

Then to the pit the Collier goes,
  To earn his daily bread;
He may be killed for aught he knows,
  And go to Christ his Head.

Then he goes under the dark shade,
  To labour with his hands;
He grows up to his living Head,
  While Jesus with him stands.

He persecuted is, we hear,
  By proud and cruel men;
Through grace divine, he does not fear
  But prays for them again.

While some do swear on his right side,
  And on his left as well;
He prays to Jesus that hath died,
  To save their souls from hell.

Though floods of troubles roll along,
  The Collier's peaceful breast;
The love of Jesus is his song,
  He on that rock doth rest.

And when the Collier's work is done,
  Then to his home he goes;
His Christian feet are swift to run
  Where milk and honey flows.

The Word of God is his delight,
  While he's with his children; [might
He loves that God whose pow'r and
  Brought him to them again.

And when instruction he has given,
  To all his family;
He earnestly solicits heav'n
  Their souls may never die.

But live to God while in this world,
  And feel their sins forgiven,
And never into hell be hurl'd
  But reign with Christ in heaven.

He not only prays that the blessing of God may rest upon himself and family, but he also prays for the extension of the Messiah's Kingdom; and his language is something like the following, viz. :—

Send thy enlight'ning Spirit, Lord,
  To all the sons of men;
And let them hear Thy quick'ning word
  And feel they're born again.

Unless Thou dost Thy pow'r display,
  Poor souls, they must be lost;
Oh! let Thy hand of justice stay;
  Consider what they cost.

They cost the blood of Thy dear Son,
  While in our world below;
We know Thou hast the work begun,
  Let ALL Thy mercy know.

POLITICS

During 1820 and 1821, when Queen Caroline was tried, acquitted and then died, and again during the agitation for reform before 1832 politics became part of the broadside repertoire. No other controversies in 'high' politics had anything like the same impact. Sabbatarian legislation and the introduction of the Police, political issues which affected the lives of the purchasers of broadsheets much more directly, frequently provided subjects for broadsides.

39 *Reviewing the blue devils*

1833. 221 × 340 mm.

Few people would now accuse the Metropolitan Police of being verminous. This cut is perhaps from G. Drake of Clare Market, who also published number 43.

40 *Caroline triumphant*

John Pitts. 1820. 197 × 137 mm.

Pitts offers a hieratic image of the Queen
on her throne. It is not a recognisable
portrait, but then it has no need to be.

41 *Principal characters in a new piece entitled The Man Wot Drives the Sovereign*

James Catnach. 1829. 360 × 327 mm.

This print, of various political figures as
stage-coach characters, is adapted from a
series of intaglio prints by W. Heath, either
directly by Catnach or at second hand
from another broadside printer, G. Drake,
who sold a very similar sheet. Catnach and
his successors reused many of the dozen
cuts on this sheet, first for further political
sheets, later as ornaments to illustrate
ballads.

40

Principal Characters in the New Piece entitled
The MAN *wot* Drives the Sovereign.

All vell at Vindsor

Does Jerry mean to start on his own account ? Them leaders seem to have it all their own way.

The Slap-up SWELL wot drives when hever he likes

ACHILLES.

Ready to set, your Honour.

The MAN wot drives the SOVEREIGN

Orange P--l

He made each felley turn his coat, And caught each rat by the tail.

The CAD to the MAN wot drives the SOVEREIGN

The Cunning Hen

I says to our Governor, says I, Keep your eye on them 'ere leaders, George, or they'll bolt with the coach.

The GUARD wot looks after the SOVEREIGN.

Paddy Whack

Cut away, ye divils, cut away—Ye'l bent them now--- Ould Ireland for ever---I Huzza !

The Regular Ou'-and-Outer wot drives the Hero

The Ould'un

I drove the Long Tail Blacks for fifty years. A drove your lad, your honour.

The MAN wot drives the OPPOSITION.

A Kow-Cumber.

I say, Jemmy All-Weather, keep your eye on them fellies of the Sovereign—they're arter no goods. See they don't prig our baggage. That coach is their vin, they think.

The MAN wots guard the OPPOSITON.

Man of all Weathers

I was once a bright lad, But now I'm a Cad.

The Cad to the Man wot drives the OPPOSITION

Once in Battersea Now in Chelsea.

Death's heads and marrow bones, are now my portion.

The MAN wot missed his mark.

A drive from Dublin

One kick from the leader floor'd me.

The MAN wot could not drive as he liked.

Long Franky.

Iused to go by the John Bull, now I goes by the Satur age.

The MAN wot owns the VESTMINISTER.

Last Stage.

These felleys drive too hard; I must carry less luggage.

JOHN BULL, broke down.

41

42

42 *The Vauxhall melodist*

T. Bloomer. Birmingham, 1820. 119 × 149 mm.

This curious sheet offers portraits of all the major figures in Caroline's
trial for adultery, as well as this cut of the illuminations at Vauxhall,
whose strongest connection with the case seems to be that a similar cut
occurs in Pitts's *Caroline triumphant*.

43 *Things not to be done on the Sabbath*

G. Drake. 1837. 309 × 241 mm.

This was number five in the series 'The Political Drama', published on the
occasion of Agnew's Sabbatarian Bill.

44

45

44 Most gracious speech of His Majesty William IV to both Houses of Parliament, November 2nd 1830

Kay (a provincial printer). 1830. 81 ×90 mm.

Other heraldic cuts are found on broadsides but they were evidently bought from high-class printers as bankrupt or surplus stock. This cut is unusual for its down-to-earth directness.

45 The Sunday Beer Bill is repealed

Anne Ryle (printed 'Rial'). 1855. 56 ×78 mm.

By the 1850s politics was presented in broadsides almost entirely in the form of topical songs. The subtle irony of this illustration is achieved with sophisticated economy.

46 A trial between right and might, or the enemies of the poor man short in weight

H. Paul. 1841. 220 × 270 mm.

This is one of the last broadsides to deal with straight 'high' politics: this role was being taken over by the illustrated papers, and the symbolic imagery which this print employs was being moderated by the more oblique, more ironic school of Punch.

47 *An attempt to exhibit the leading events of the Queen's life*

James Catnach. 1821. 106 × 180 mm.

This is an adaptation for political purposes of an elegiac image, occuring both in 'high' art and in the broadside repertoire, of the tomb shaded by trees and attended by more or less symbolic mourners.

48 *The managers' last kick, or the distruction* [sic] *of the boroughmongers*

J.V. Quick. 1832. 194 × 212 mm.

This cut, probably done by Quick himself, owes much to *The Pigs Possessed*, executed in 1807 by Gillray.

HUMOUR

Broadside humour is as difficult to define
or classify as any other form of humour.
Slapstick, mock heroics, irony, situation
comedy, smutty jokes, and visual and
verbal puns were all employed. The cuts
from humorous broadsides do not, for
the most part, depend very directly on the
models of intaglio caricature or of *Punch*
and its ilk; they succeed in portraying the
urban poor, who are at once the audience
and the butt of most of the jokes, in a
direct and unpatronising way.

49 *The oyster man*

John Pitts. Undated, perhaps from the late
1820s. 103 × 148 mm.

This is Pitts's attempt to cash in on the great success of
a comic sheet by Catnach, *The dandy dogs' meat man.*

50 The new Marriage Act

James Catnach. 1822. 43 × 175 mm.

This cut derives, probably at second hand, from a Rowlandson aquatint of 1788, *The Cart Race*. Compared with Batchelar's (51), Catnach's imagery is slick, up to date and allusive. Although he had considerable success with a few such novelties, most of his humorous broadsides were far humbler and more traditional.

51 A general summons to all hornified fumblers to assemble for horn fair

T. Batchelar. Undated, but between 1817 and 1828. 140 × 170 mm.

An image stocked with the ancient emblems of the war between the sexes.

52 *Crim con extraordinary*

J. Paul. Undated, but from the early 1840s. 134 × 192 mm.

The cuckolded husband returns unexpectedly, the faithless wife waits in confusion, and the happy apprentice makes an undignified exit. The cut tells us almost all we need to know, and leaves the text free to concentrate on verbal humour rather than on the telling of a story.

53 *The Charlies' holiday, or the tears of London at the funeral of Tom and Jerry*

James Catnach. 1823. 83 × 238 mm.

Pierce Egan's story of Tom and Jerry, the country bucks in London for a spree, had been turned into a play. When it closed, a mock funeral was held. Catnach reports it here as he had reported the couple's earlier adventures, which had included the teasing and beating of the nightwatchmen, nick-named the Charlies.

53

BALLADS

The imagery of ballads is more difficult to date and to categorise than any other. It can be divided into two sorts: the small images which decorated slip ballads and for which old blocks were quite adequate, and a smaller range of cuts, done specifically to illustrate a particular song, which were usually larger and more elaborate. Naturally these were used later to head yards of ballads. Although slip-ballad imagery was replenished by cuts from other branches of the trade, it did not become outdated, and so despite the fact that most of the small images reproduced here come from unnamed printers and that many of them probably originated in the eighteenth century, they are in every sense nineteenth-century images.

The Rural Songster.

54 *The rural songster*

James Catnach. Before 1834.
113 × 171 mm.

The images used by the majority of ballad printers were less striking than those used by Pitts, but in this sheet Catnach uses dozens of birds to produce an unusual and puzzling image.

55 *The distracted maiden*

63 × 76 mm.

A spectacular image of madness.
Reproduced × 1.5.

56 *The Panthen*

John Pitts. After 1819.
195 × 158 mm.

Whatever its original significance, this figure,
atop its yard of ballads, must have attracted
considerable attention.

55

THE PANTHEN.

56

57 *A new love song*

37 × 45 mm.

58 *The wild rover, a new song*

51 × 57 mm.

Here one is struck by the boldness of the design
and cutting rather than by its connection with this
ballad.

59 *The disconsolate lover*

34 × 43 mm.

60 *The sailor's welcome home*

57 × 51 mm.

61 *The disconsolate sailor*

49 × 61 mm.

Illustrations to nautical ballads were usually of ships.

62 *A new song, called The Distressed Sons of Erin*

37 × 43 mm.

Apart from the fact that it has been printed upside
down, this cut is of interest because it is discernably a
woodcut rather than a wood-engraving: the grain is
clearly visible.

63 *The Monteuch wedding*

32 × 36 mm.

This ballad with its charming little bird, *The
disconsolate lover* where the pot and its lid form a
delightful design, and *The sailor's welcome home*, where
instead of a sailor a kilted Scot is depicted, show how
hard it can be to make connections between text and
image in slip ballads. Sometimes, as with *The
disconsolate sailor* or *A new love song*, an association
between text and image can be discerned, but these
three leave the present author baffled.

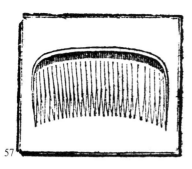

57

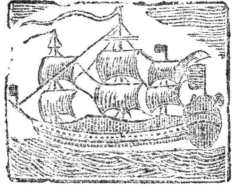

61

58

59

A New Song, Called, The

Distressed

Sons of Erin !

62

60

63

64 *Rory O'More*

Elizabeth Hodges. After 1841. 50 × 90 mm.

Elizabeth Hodges, who had been Pitts's housekeeper, took over his business on his death, selling old stock, reprinting favourites and publishing a limited range of new items. Women did not generally set up in the printing trade on their own, but they frequently and successfully ran printing shops which had been bequeathed to them as heirs or widows, and the success with which they managed them indicates the extent to which they had collaborated with their husbands, fathers, lovers or brothers, probably more as administrators than as compositors, block-cutters or press-workers.

Reproduced × 1.5.

65 *The champion*

212 × 149 mm.

Prize-fights formed a staple of broadside imagery. This is rather a good cut: the fact that the block has been smashed perhaps accounts for its presence on a song sheet.

66 *The wanderer*

John Pitts. After 1819. 97 × 117 mm.

A good example of the romantic landscape
style of illustration, showing the influence
of Bewick.

67 *Kate of Colebrook Dale*

John Pitts. Before 1819. 101 × 135 mm.

This, together with numbers 66 and 68, were cut for Pitts when he was trying to compete against intaglio printers such as Laurie and Whittle for the luxury end of the ballad market. This particular cut offers the curious combination of an idyllic pastoral scene and an industrial landscape with mines (whose shafts are shown schematically) and coking ovens.

68 *The exciseman*

John Pitts. After 1819. 101 × 125 mm.

This song was originally published as an etched song sheet, one of the Laurie and Whittle series. Pitts copied the song but produced an entirely new illustration for it. Later he used the block for a long half sheet of songs, *The jovial fellows*.

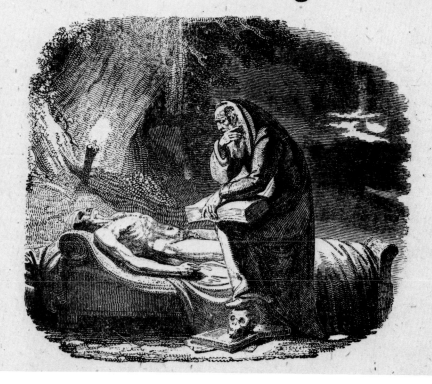

69 *The frightful and dreadful murders at Denham in Buckinghamshire*

92 × 107 mm.

This topical ballad is illustrated with an image which derives from such paintings as *The Death of Atala* by Girodet.

ALMANACKS AND CHRISTMAS SHEETS

Almanacks and Christmas sheets were both eighteenth-century forms which remained basically unchanged in the nineteenth. Bellmen, lamplighters and newsmen distributed sheets of verses in return for Christmas tips. Christmas sheets often included comic caricatures, riddles and games, as well as cuts of jollification. The imagery of prophetic almanacks, with its mixture of politics, religion, magic and ancient history, is difficult to understand today: much of it was probably intended to be obscure.

70 *Gaslamplighter's poem*

J. V. Quick. Undated, perhaps *c*.1822. 135 × 153 mm.

This vivid and detailed cut, from a sheet showing the perils and hardships of the gaslamplighters' trade, is without parallel in sheets showing those of the bellmen's trade.

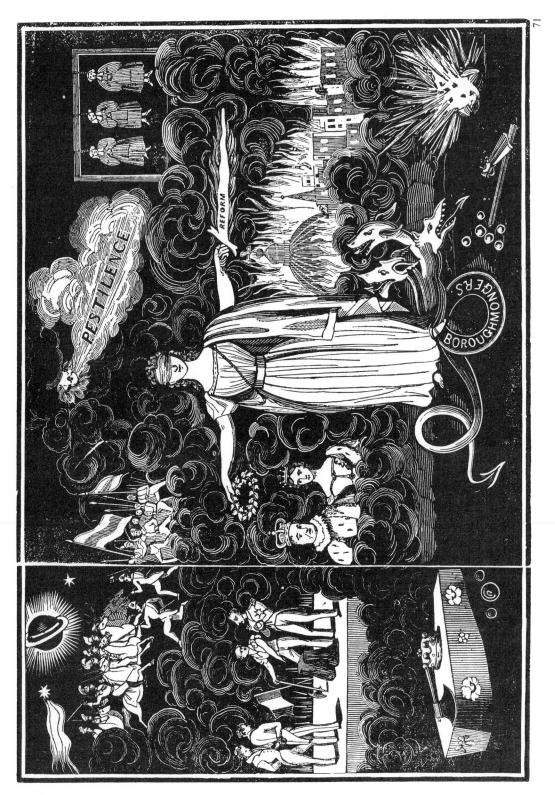

71 Prophetic annual for 1832

S. Robins. 1832. 178 × 254 mm.

This image is filled with more political references than most, but then 1832 was politically a highly eventful year.

72 The particulars of Twelfth Night, and the drawing of king and queen

John Pitts. After 1819. 149 × 200 mm.

This cut, which Pitts almost certainly copied from Catnach, has been simplified and abstracted in the process, and the result is an image of wierd, dark beauty.

73 *A copy of verses for 1811, humbly presented to all my worthy masters and mistresses in the liberty of Saffron Hill, Hatton Garden and Ely Rents*

John Bayley. 1811. 125 × 275 mm.

Different representations of the group portrait of a bellman and two watchmen appeared at the top of most bellmen's sheets.

MORALITIES

The boundaries between execution sheets,
moralities and straight religious sheets are
sometimes hard to draw, yet what Pepys called
'Penny Godlinesses' do deserve a place apart.
Improving narratives of folly, cruelty or
licentiousness and their punishment, and of
virtue and its reward were popular, as were a
limited range of variations on the theme of the
imminence of death. Symbolic representations
of the nature of human existence also occur,
and it is only among such moralities that one
finds parallels with the abundant popular
imagery of Continental Europe.

74 *The wandering Jew*

James Catnach. Before 1834. 145 × 175 mm.

This, one of the commonest themes in Continental popular imagery, is
rare in the English broadside repertoire.

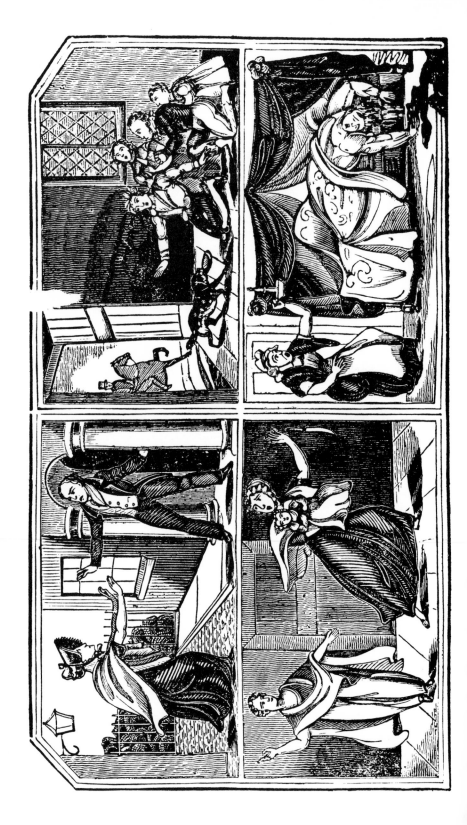

75 Comfort to the afflicted, or the wondrous works of God shown to the widow and fatherless

James Catnach. Before 1834. 115 × 200 mm.

A widow turns to the parish for help which is refused by the churchwarden. She is on the point of putting her life and the lives of her children to an end when an angel stops her. Help arrives, and the churchwarden is found miraculously and horribly dead in bed.

108

76 *A full and particular account of John Jobling, a gentleman's son*

James Catnach. c.1832. 114 × 192 mm.

John Jobling dissipated his fortune on good living, whoring and gambling, and made the grave mistake of being a blasphemous unbeliever to boot. The devils who here carry him away from the roulette table are like many who occur in broadside imagery. The easy co-existence of representations of the natural and supernatural worlds is typical.

110

THE AFFECTIONATE
DAUGHTER

ving an Account of Antony Moiras, a rich and powerful Gentleman, who, for some treasonable offence against the State, was sentenced to be Starved to Death in a dismal, horrible Dun-
geon—shewing how his Life was most wonderfully preserved by the Milk from his Daughter's Breast.

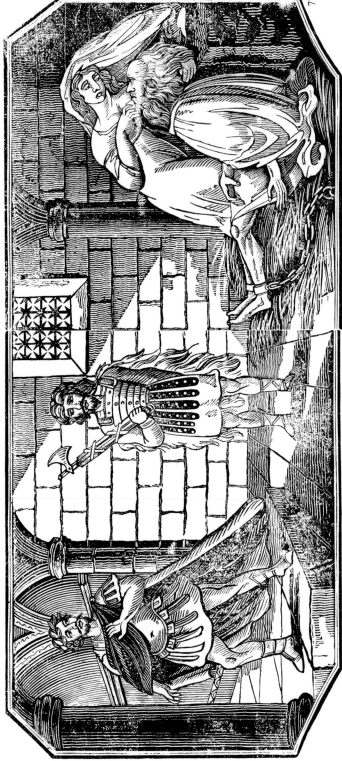

77 The affectionate daughter

James Catnach. Before 1834. 148 × 330 mm.

Antony Molina, imprisoned without food for crimes against the state, is saved by his daughter's milk. Her devotion impresses the king and wins Molina a pardon.

78 The twelve stages of human life

William Walker and Sons. Otley; undated, but after 1862. 170 × 340 mm.

This was copied from a Catnach print and was a common image in broadsides, having eighteenth-century antecedents in England and a longer history and an even greater success on the Continent.

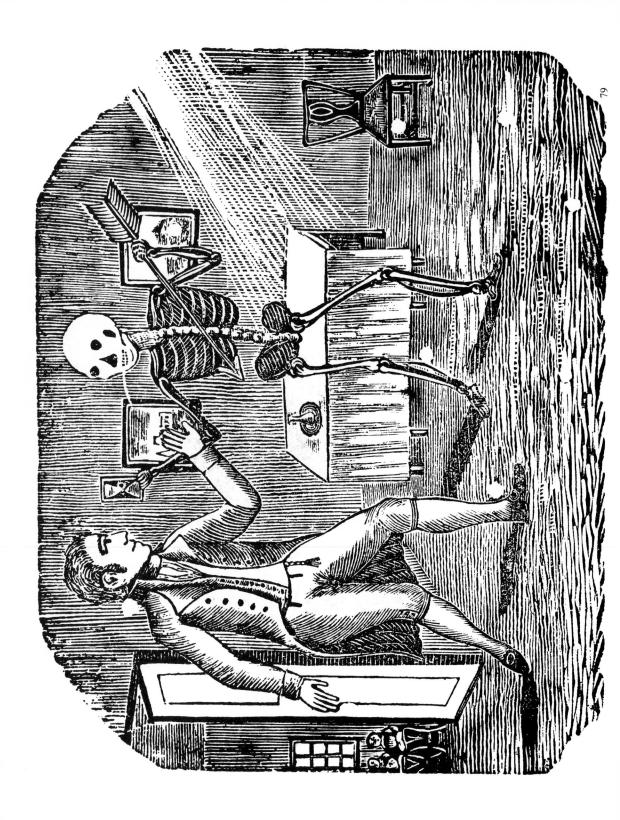

79 The great concern of every Christian

152 × 185 mm.

The wood for this block seems to have come from a beam out of a building: notice its half-squared shape and the nine or ten death-watch beetle holes in it. Woodworm frequently attacked blocks in store at the printers, but death-watch beetle preferred whole timbers.

80 The dying infidel, or the judgments of God displayed in the awful end of miserable sinners

T. Ford. Chesterfield. 155 × 320 mm.

This version of the *memento mori* appears to have been copied from some late eighteenth-century painting or high-quality engraving: its composition is unusually sophisticated.

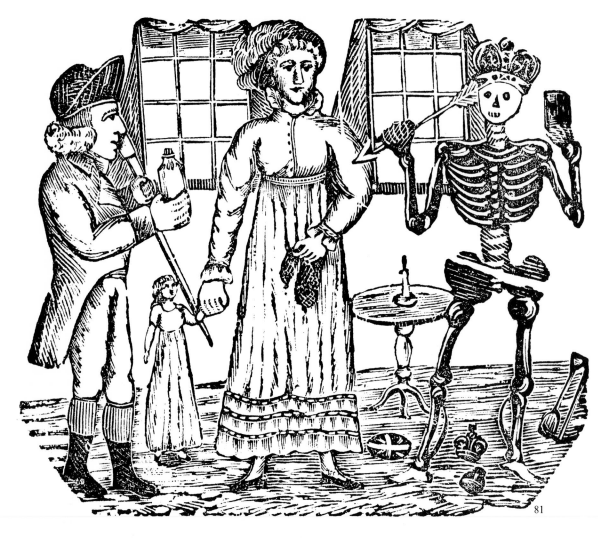

81

81 *The messenger of mortality, or a dialogue between death and the lady*

W. Carrall. York, *c*.1818. 147 × 175 mm.

At various levels of sophistication this cut and numbers 79 and 80 all employ the traditional iconography of death: the hourglass, the skeleton, with a javelin rather than a scythe, the disruption of domestic bliss and the hollowness of human vanities.

82 *The tree of life*

W. Fortey. *c*.1860. 318 × 248 mm.

This block had previously been used by Catnach, who probably derived it from a very similar etched image sold by Batchelar at the beginning of the century.

114

83 *The village bell*

James Catnach. After 1834. 91 × 162 mm.
Catnach's ideal village.

RELIGION

Prayer sheets, hymn sheets, and inspirational and devotional sheets of many kinds were produced for the broadside market. Illustrations were taken from Bible stories, while the symbolism of the Book of Revelations combined with that of various magical traditions to produce a complex set of emblems and signs for heaven, hell, the structure of the universe, the meaning of life and the events of the Last Judgement. Religious imagery was freer and more varied than that of any other broadside form, perhaps because the sale of sheets offering hymns, set prayers and Biblical instruction to the broadside market had no strong eighteenth-century roots, and printers were thus able – perhaps even forced – to seek models in another successful 'popular' religious art, baroque religious painting.

THE PLOUGHBOY'S DREAM.

84

84 *The ploughboy's dream and farmer's prayer*

W. Fortey. *c*.1860. 77 × 155 mm.

An unusual cut, which closely copies one used by Catnach's immediate successors, Paul and Co. It has affinities with the transfer-printed illustrations to be found on Sunderland and other English provincial pottery of the period.

85 *The dying pilgrim*

James Catnach. *c*.1832. 100 × 75 mm.

Engravings by Rembrandt and others of Rubens' *Descent from the Cross*, from Antwerp Cathedral, must surely have provided Catnach's source for this cut.

85

86 *Nativity of Christ, with hymns for Christmas*

John Pitts. After 1819. 94 × 155 mm.

Nativities and Crucifixions understandably show the strongest and most
consistent influence of 'high' art in the whole of the broadside repertoire.
This is a particularly attractive example.

87 *The fall of man*

James Catnach. Before 1834. 145 × 340 mm.

This cut is taken from a sheet with very little
text, most of the space being given to a variety
of devotional images.

88 Moses in the bulrushes

John Pitts. After 1819. 159 × 222 mm.

This cut is unusually fresh and is a mixture of topographical artlessness and sophistication.

89 The last day! Prepare to meet thy God!

James Catnach. Before 1834. 116 × 330 mm.

Notice that the lower right-hand corner of this print is lighter than the rest, which is evidence that at this date (probably c.1830) Catnach was still using dabbers instead of ink rollers. In this, as in every respect, broadside printers saved money by refusing to invest in labour-saving technology.

89

124

90 *The golden chain of salvation*

James Catnach. After 1834.
295 × 340 mm.

This image carries a great deal of precise information about the next world but none about this. It provokes contemplation rather than action and is therefore well adapted to a stable society. As long as stability remained the dominant feature of social relations, the broadside prospered; as change replaced stability as the norm, the broadside and its distinctive imagery disappeared.

91 *Christmas drawing near at hand*

Ann Batchelar. 1832–6. 102 × 97 mm.

This cut, and cuts 90 and 92, represent the strong tradition of symbolic imagery in the broadside repertoire, which is also found in illustrations to almanacks.

92 *Christmas drawing near at hand*

John Pitts. Possibly 1822.
206 × 163 mm.

Pitts could afford to be much more lavish than T. Batchelar's ageing widow. This is the largest of six cuts on his sheet of this subject, whereas Batchelar's has only the one.

93

93 *The Virgin Mary*

James Catnach. After 1834. 135 × 85 mm.

There are two other cuts of roughly the same size on this sheet, one of the Virgin, and one of the Crucifixion. All derive from seventeenth-century Italian religious painting. Disley, a rival printer, copied this cut and that of the Virgin for a sheet of the same title.

Further Reading

This list includes books of direct relevance to this study rather than works which have contributed to an understanding of the social and cultural history of the period. I should like to record one fundamental intellectual debt to William Ivin's *Prints and Visual Communication* (Routledge and Kegan Paul, 1953). Place of publication is London, unless otherwise specified.

Altick, R., *Victorian Studies in Scarlet*, Dent, 1972.

Hindley, C. (comp.), '*The Catnach Press*', *A Collection of the Books and Woodcuts of James Catnach, Late of Seven Dials, Printer* (with an account of his life), Reeves and Turner, 1869.
The Life and Times of James Catnach, late of Seven Dials, Ballad-monger, 1878.
The History of the Catnach Press, at Berwick-upon-Tweed, Alnwick and Newcastle-upon-Tyne, in Northumberland and Seven Dials, London, C. Hindley, 1886.

James, L. (ed.), *Print and the People 1819–1851*, Harmondsworth, Allen Lane, 1976.

Lindley, K., *The Woodblock Engravers*, Newton Abbot, David and Charles, 1970.

Laver, J. (ed.), *L'Imagerie populaire anglaise*, Paris, Electra, 1976.

Mayhew, H., *London Labour and The London Poor*, 4 vols, 1861–2.

Shepard, L., *The Broadside Ballad: a Study in Origins and Meanings*, Herbert Jenkins, 1962.
John Pitts, Ballad Printer, of Seven Dials, London 1765–1844, with a short account of his Predecessors in the Ballad and Chapbook Trade, Pinner, Private Libraries Association, 1969.
The History of Street Literature. The Story of Broadside Ballads, Chapbooks, Proclamations, News-sheets, Election Bills, Tracts, Pamphlets, Cocks, Catchpennies and other Ephemera, Newton Abbot, David and Charles, 1973.

Twyman, M., *Printing 1770–1970, an Illustrated History of its Development and Uses in England*, Eyre and Spottiswoode, 1970.

For a glimpse of the parallels and striking differences between English and some Continental popular imageries, *French Popular Imagery*, the Arts Council catalogue of the exhibition held at Hayward Gallery in 1974, is useful.